Serial Shifting for the Viola

by Cassia Harvey

CHP203

6403 N. 6th Street
Philadelphia, PA 19126
www.charveypublications.com

Cassia Harvey

3

4

7

8

3

4

15

16

19

20

1

2

23

24

27

28

31

32

35

36

7

38

D string

9

40

1

42

43

44

45

46

47

30

48

49

50

51

52

53

54

56

58

59

1

62

63

Fourth Position for the Viola

1

by Cassia Harvey

A. First Shifting on the A String

B. First Shifting on the D String